Cornerstones of Freedom

The Emancipation Proclamation

Brendan January

CHILDREN'S PRESS®
A Division of Grolier Publishing
New York • London • Hong Kong • Sydney
Danbury, Connecticut

Library of Congress Cataloging-in-Publication Data

January, Brendan, 1972–
  The Emancipation Proclamation / by Brendan January.
    p. cm.— (Cornerstones of freedom)
  Includes index.
  Summary: Tells the story of the document which eventually led to the passage of the Thirteenth Amendment and relates the role of President Lincoln in freeing the slaves.
  ISBN: 0-516-20394-0 (lib. bdg.) 0-516-26226-2 (pbk.)
  1. United States. President (1861–1865: Lincoln). Emancipation Proclamation—Juvenile literature. 2. Lincoln, Abraham, 1809–1865—Juvenile literature. 3. Slaves—Emancipation— United States—Juvenile literature. 4. United States—Politics and government—1861–1865—Juvenile literature. [1. Lincoln, Abraham, 1809–1865. 2. Slavery. 3. United States—Politics and government— 1861–1865.] I. Title. II. Series.
E453.J36 1997
973.7—dc21
                      96-50145
                      CIP
                      AC

THE EMANCIPATION PROCLAMATION

Whereas, On the twenty-second day of September, in the year of our Lord one thousand eight hundred and sixty-two, a proclamation was issued by the President of the United States, containing, among other things, the following, to wit:

"That on the first day of January, in the year of our Lord one thousand eight hundred and sixty-three, [all persons held as slav]es within any State, or de[signated part of a State, the] people whereof shall then [be in rebellion against th]e United States, shall be then, [thenceforward, and fore]ver, free, and the Executive [Government of the Unit]ed States, including the mili[tary and naval authorit]y thereof, will recognize and [maintain the freedom of suc]h persons, and will do no [act or acts to repress suc]h persons, or any of them, in [any efforts they may m]ake for their actual freedom.

[That the Executive will,] on the first day of January [aforesaid, by proclamati]on, designate the States and [parts of States, if any,] in which the people therein, [respectively, shall the]n be in rebellion against the [United States; and the f]act that any State, or the [people thereof, shall on] that day, be, in good faith, [represented in the Cong]ress of the United States, by [members chosen thereto] at elections, wherein a ma[jority of the qualified vo]ters of such State shall have [participated, shall, in th]e absence of strong counter[vailing testimony, be dee]med conclusive evidence that [such State and the peopl]e thereof are not then in re[bellion against the Unite]d States."

[Now, therefore I, ABR]AHAM LINCOLN, President of [the United States, by vir]tue of the power in me vested [as Commander-in-Chief o]f the Army and Navy of the [United States in time of a]ctual armed rebellion against [the authority and gover]nment of the United States, [and as a fit and necessary] war measure for suppressing the said rebellion, do, on this, the first day of January, in the year of our Lord one thousand eight hundred and sixty-three, and, in accordance with my purpose so to do, publicly proclaim, for the full period of one hundred days from the day first above mentioned, or-der and designate as the States and parts of States wherein the people thereof respectively are this day in rebellion against the United States, the follow-ing, to wit: Arkansas, Texas, Louisiana (except the parishes of St. Bernard, Plaquemines, Jeffer-son, St. James, Ascension, Assumption, Terre-bonne, Lafourche, St. Martin, and Orleans, includ-ing the city of New Orleans), Mississippi, Alabama, Florida, Georgia, South Carolina, North Carolina, and Virginia (except the forty-eight counties des-ignated as West Virginia, and also the counties of Berkley, Accomac, Northampton, Elizabeth City, York, Princess Ann, and Norfolk, including the cities of Norfolk and Portsmouth), and which ex-cepted parts are for the present left precisely as if the proclamation were not issued.

And, by virtue of the power and for the purpose aforesaid, I do order and declare that all persons held as slaves within the said designated States and parts of said States, are, and henceforward shall be, free; and that the Executive Government of the United States, including the military and naval authorities thereof, will recognize and maintain the freedom of said persons.

And I hereby enjoin upon the people so declared to be free, to abstain from all violence, unless in neces-sary self-defence, and I recommend to them that in all cases, when allowed, they labor faithfully for reason-able wages. And I further declare and make known, that such persons, of suitable condition, will be re-ceived into the armed service of the United States, to garrison forts, positions, stations and other places, and to man vessels of all sorts in the said service. And upon this act, sincerely believed to be an act of justice, warranted by the constitution, upon military necessity, I invoke the considerate judgment of mankind, and the gracious favor of Almighty God.

In witness whereof I have hereunto set my hand, and caused the seal of the United States to be affixed.

[L. S.] Done at the city of Washington, this, the first day of January, in the year of our Lord one thou-sand eight hundred and sixty-three, and of the inde-pendence of the United States of America the eighty seventh.

A. Lincoln

Proclaim Liberty throughout all the Land unto all the Inhabitants thereof. Lev. XXV.X.

In the early 1800s, the young United States began to divide into two separate societies. In the North, thriving factories and railroads expanded into the unsettled West. Millions of people emigrated from Europe to the United States. Most of them settled in the North to take advantage of the vibrant economy. From Maine to Minnesota, cities and factories grew up out of the fields and forests.

Much of the Northern economy depended on goods that were produced in factories.

Crops grown on farms and plantations drove the Southern economy.

In the South, small farms and giant plantations covered the landscape. The Southern
economy depended on the growth of crops,
such as cotton. To keep the plantations
working, the owners employed slaves.
Southerners believed that without slavery,
their entire economy would collapse.

By the 1840s and 1850s, many Northerners
considered slavery immoral and cruel. These

men and women were called abolitionists. They wondered how a nation that proclaimed that "all men are created equal" in its Declaration of Independence could practice slavery. As a result, they pressured the federal government in Washington, D.C., to ban slavery throughout the nation.

Southerners believed that their economy would not survive without the use of slave labor on their plantations.

Southerners reacted to the Northerners' criticism with outrage. "Since when can a Northern state tell a Southern state how to run its business?" they cried. Slaveowners considered their slaves to be property, and the U.S. Constitution, which had been adopted in 1787, protected the citizen's right to own property. Many Southerners threatened to secede from, or leave, the Union. They wanted to form a separate country where slavery was allowed. From the halls of Congress to the smallest town square, the issue was the topic of heated debate.

In 1860, Abraham Lincoln ran for the presidency of the United States as the Republican nominee. The Republican party opposed the expansion of slavery into the country's western territories. But Southerners feared that the Republican party was

Abraham Lincoln

an abolitionist party that would
forbid slavery in every state. The
Southerners vowed to secede if
the Republicans gained power.

   When Abraham Lincoln won the
presidential election in 1860, he
tried to reassure the Southerners.
"I will not touch slavery where it
exists, I will only prevent it from
entering the Western territories,"
he said. But most of the people in
the South did not believe him, and several states
seceded. South Carolina was the first state to
secede, followed by Georgia, Alabama, Florida,
Mississippi, and Louisiana. Later, North Carolina,
Arkansas, Texas, Tennessee, and Virginia followed.

*Badges and ribbons
were worn by the
supporters of
Lincoln's
presidential
campaign.*

*During 1860–1861,
most of the
Southern states
left the Union.*

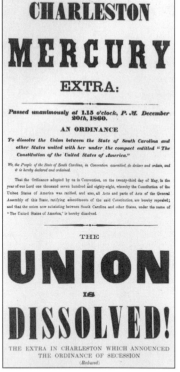

On December 20, 1860, South Carolina was the first state to leave the Union.

In February 1861, six Southern states organized into the Confederate States of America. They declared themselves to be a new country, and they seized forts and property that belonged to the United States government. President Lincoln vowed to defend the federal authority of the United States with force, if necessary. In April 1861, the Confederates attacked Fort Sumter in Charleston Harbor, South Carolina, and the Civil War began.

During the first year of the war, President Lincoln tried to convince the Southern states to return to the Union peacefully. His main priority was to save the Union, so he carefully avoided any action that threatened slavery. Lincoln believed that the Confederates would rejoin the Union when they realized that he would not change their way of life. To demon-

The Civil War officially began on April 12, 1861, with the Confederate bombardment of Fort Sumter in Charleston Harbor, South Carolina.

strate his attitude, Lincoln ordered Union generals who had freed Southern slaves to return them to their owners. In a letter to a Union officer, Lincoln wrote, "liberating slaves . . . will alarm our Southern Union friends, and turn them against us."

Lincoln's policy toward slavery disappointed many Northern Republicans. They had voted for Lincoln because they believed that he would challenge the slave system. Lincoln, however, believed that the Constitution gave him no authority to abolish slavery. The Republicans argued that the Constitution did grant the president special powers during a war. Now that the country was fighting a civil war, they reasoned, Lincoln could use those special powers to abolish slavery.

Congress constantly debated the issue of slavery and its importance to the Civil War.

Lincoln gave other reasons why he did not want to free the slaves. He was especially worried about the army. Lincoln knew that many of the soldiers were fighting to save the Union, not to free the slaves. He worried that the soldiers might become angry and withdraw from the army. It would be hopeless to try to fight the war without an army. The president was right. Some white Northerners believed that if the slaves were freed, they would come north and take Northern jobs. Many of these workers were fighting in the Union army. Lincoln feared that the Union army would not have enough soldiers to fight the war if he freed the slaves.

Lincoln had other worries, as well. Some slave states—Delaware, Missouri, Kentucky, and Maryland—remained loyal to the Union. They were called border states because they sat on the border between the Northern states and the Southern states. The Union cause needed the border states to stay in the Union. Lincoln believed that if he threatened slavery, then the border states might join the Confederacy. If Maryland seceded, then Washington, D.C., and the White House, could become the Confederate capital.

Lincoln wrestled with the issue of slavery throughout the winter of 1861–1862. In the spring of 1862, General Robert E. Lee and the Confederate army drove the Union army out of southern Virginia. As a result, people throughout the North began to lose confidence that they could win the war. The Union army needed more soldiers, but fewer men volunteered to fight. With the situation growing desperate, Lincoln decided to emancipate the slaves.

On July 22, 1862, Lincoln gathered his top advisers to the White House. These men made up Lincoln's cabinet and he always discussed important decisions with them. When they all were seated, Lincoln began the meeting, telling them, "Gentlemen, it appears that we must change our tactics or lose the game. It has become apparent we must free the slaves to win the war." Lincoln explained that he was committed to his decision, but he wanted to hear the advisers' opinions on the idea of emancipation. Lincoln read aloud the ending of his rough draft of the Emancipation Proclamation:

> *all persons held as slaves within any state or states, wherein the constitutional authority of the United States shall not then be practically recognized, submitted to, and maintained, shall then, thenceforward, and forever, be free.*

The proclamation stunned the cabinet members. No president had ever acted so drastically in the history of the United States. They did not know how to react. Lincoln's closest advisor, William Seward, urged the president to wait before he issued the proclamation. "If you sign the proclamation now, everyone will think you're doing it out of fear," he argued. "Critics of the proclamation can call it a move made out of weakness. The people will see it as a last shriek of desperation. The Union army must win a battle before you can issue the proclamation."

William Seward advised President Lincoln to wait until the Union won a battle before making the proclamation public.

Lincoln listened to Seward's advice. He returned the proclamation to his desk drawer and waited. Because the Union army had few victories in the war, Lincoln worried that the chance to issue his proclamation might never arrive.

The months of July and August passed. Lincoln waited anxiously for a Union victory. In September 1862, General Lee and the Confederate army pushed into the border states when they invaded Maryland. Lincoln spent many nervous nights at the war department in

General Lee and the Confederate army invaded Maryland on September 17, 1862.

Washington, D.C., hoping to hear good news. On September 17, the Union and Confederate armies clashed at Antietam Creek in western Maryland. Both armies suffered more than ten thousand casualties in the single day of fighting, but the Union army was victorious.

The Union army drove the Confederates out of Maryland at the Battle of Antietam.

On September 22, 1862, Lincoln read the Emancipation Proclamation to the public for the first time. Lincoln also declared that if the rebelling states did not return to the Union by January 1, 1863, then slavery would be illegal in the South forever. But the Emancipation Proclamation did not abolish slavery everywhere. The loyal border states did not have to free their slaves. Lincoln also allowed slaveowners who supported the Union to keep their slaves.

In the South, the proclamation outraged Jefferson Davis, the president of the Confederacy. He claimed that Lincoln was trying to cause a bloody slave rebellion against white masters. He urged the Confederacy to fight even harder for independence from the Union. Southern newspapers also expressed their fury at Lincoln. An editorial in the *Richmond (Virginia) Enquirer*

Jefferson Davis, president of the Confederacy, was angered by Lincoln's Emancipation Proclamation. In this address to the citizens of the Northern states, Davis announced that "the proper condition of the negro is slavery."

AN ADDRESS TO THE PEOPLE OF THE FREE STATES

BY THE

PRESIDENT OF THE SOUTHERN CONFEDERACY.

RICHMOND, January 5, 1863.

Citizens of the non-slave-holding States of America, swayed by peaceable motives, I have used all my influence, often thereby endangering my position as the President of the Southern Confederacy, to have the unhappy conflict now existing between my people and yourselves, governed by those well established international rules, which heretofore have softened the asperities which necessarily are the concomitants of a state of belligerency, but all my efforts in the premises have heretofore been unavailing. Now, therefore, I am compelled *e necessitati rei* to employ a measure, which most willingly I would have omitted to do, regarding, as I always must, State Rights, as the very organism of politically associated society.

For nearly two years my people have been defending their inherent rights—their political, social and religious rights against the speculators of New England and their allies in the States heretofore regarded as conservative. The people of the Southern Confederacy have—making sacrifices such as the modern world has never witnessed—patiently, but determinedly, stood between their homeinterests and the well paid, well fed and well clad mercenaries of the Abolitionists, and I need not say that they have nobly vindicated the good name of American citizens. Heretofore, the warfare has been conducted by white men—peers, scions of the same stock; but the programme has been changed, and your rulers despairing of a triumph by the employment of white men, have degraded you and themselves, by inviting the co-operation of the black race. Thus, while they deprecate the intervention of white men—the French and the English—in behalf of the Southern Confederacy, they, these Abolitionists, do not hesitate to invoke the intervention of the African race in favor of the North.

The time has, therefore, come when a becoming respect for the good opinion of the civilized world impels me to set forth the following facts:—

First. Abraham Lincoln, the President of the Non-Slaveholding States, has issued his proclamation, declaring the slaves within the limits of the Southern Confederacy to be free.

Second. Abraham Lincoln has declared that the slaves so emancipated may be used in the Army and Navy, now under his control, by which he means to employ, against the Free People of the South, insurrectionary measures, the inevitable tendency of which will be to inaugurate a Servile War, and thereby prove destructive, in a great measure, to slave property.

Now, therefore, as a compensatory measure, I do hereby issue the following Address to the People of the Non-Slaveholding States:—

On and after February 22, 1863, all free negroes within the limits of the Southern Confederacy shall be placed on the slave status, and be deemed to be chattels, they and their issue forever.

All negroes who shall be taken in any of the States in which slavery does not now exist, in the progress of our arms, shall be adjudged, immediately after such capture, to occupy the slave status, and in all States which shall be vanquished by our arms, all free negroes shall, *ipso facto*, be reduced to the condition of helotism, so that the respective normal conditions of the white and black races may be ultimately placed on a permanent basis, so as to prevent the public peace from being thereafter endangered.

Therefore, while I would not ignore the conservative policy of the Slave States, namely, that a Federal Government cannot, without violating the fundamental principles of a Constitution, interfere with the internal policy of several States; since, however, Abraham Lincoln has seen fit to ignore the Constitution he has solemnly sworn to support, it ought not to be considered polemically or politically improper in me to vindicate the position which has been, at an early day of this Southern republic, assumed by the Confederacy, namely, that slavery is the corner-stone of a Western Republic. It is not necessary for me to elaborate this proposition. I may merely refer, in passing, to the prominent fact, that the South is emphatically a producing section of North America; this is equally true of the West and Northwest, the people of which have been mainly dependent on the South for the consumption of their products. The other States, in which slavery does not exist, have occupied a middle position, as to the South, West and Northwest. The States of New England, from which all complicated difficulties have arisen, owe their greatness and power to the free suffrages of all other sections of North America; and yet, as is now evident, they have, from the adoption of the Federal Constitution, waged a persistent warfare against the interests of all the other States of the old Union. The great centre of their opposition has been Slavery, while the annual statistics of their respective State Governments abundantly prove that they entertain within all their boundaries fewer negroes than any single State which does not tolerate slavery.

In view of these facts, and conscientiously believing that the proper condition of the negro is slavery, or a complete subjection to the white man,—and entertaining the belief that the day is not distant when the old Union will be restored with slavery nationally declared to be the proper condition of all of African descent,—and in view of the future harmony and progress of all the States of America, I have been induced to issue this address, so that there may be no misunderstanding in the future.   JEFFERSON DAVIS.

Richmond Enquirer Print.

asked, "What shall we call him? Coward, assassin, savage, murderer of women and babies? Or shall we consider them all as embodied in the word fiend, and call him Lincoln, the Fiend?"

Protected by their armies, the Confederates defied Lincoln. The Emancipation Proclamation was a meaningless piece of paper unless the Union armies liberated the slaves through force. Millions of slaves continued to work as usual. Lincoln and his advisers estimated that at first the proclamation freed only about two hundred thousand of the more than four million slaves in the South.

Secession ribbons (left, below) were worn regularly by citizens who supported the Southern Confederacy.

Many slaves met secretly to spread the word that they were free.

But the Emancipation Proclamation affected the South in other ways. Despite the frantic attempts by white Southerners to keep the news from the slaves, word of the proclamation spread like wildfire through the slave population. Unable to wait for the South to be defeated, many slaves freed themselves by fleeing to nearby Union armies. As Lincoln had hoped, the South lost many laborers, and plantations struggled to produce food for the Confederate army.

Slaves who could not wait for the Civil War to end escaped to freedom and sought to enlist in the Union army.

The Emancipation Proclamation also stated that former slaves "will be received into the armed service of the United States to garrison forts, positions, stations and other places." This meant that black soldiers could fight in the Union army. Lincoln hoped that the former slaves would help the Union war effort. He was not disappointed. Soon, eager black recruits filled many regiments in the Union army. Lincoln wrote, "Freedom has given us two hundred thousand men raised on southern soil."

Regiments of black soldiers fought bravely, both for their own freedom and for the preservation of the Union.

In the Northern states, however, many people rejected the proclamation with disgust. White citizens believed that they were fighting to save the Union, not to free the slaves. One Northern politician cried, "I told you so; can't you see this is an Abolition war and nothing else?" The *New York Daybook* called the proclamation "a criminal wrong, and an act of national suicide." A Union soldier declared, "As soon as this war stops being about the Union, and starts being about slavery, I'm going home!"

But other Northerners welcomed the idea of black soldiers fighting for the Union and recognized the benefits of the proclamation. Influential newspaper editors praised the president. Horace Greeley of the *New York Tribune* exclaimed, "God bless Abraham Lincoln." Joseph Medill of the *Chicago Tribune* called the document "the greatest proclamation ever issued by man." Thousands of letters poured into the White House. A letter from Erie, Pennsylvania, read, "God Bless you for the word you have spoken!" In major cities, crowds celebrated with bonfires and rallies. Lincoln was pleased by these signs of support, but his greatest worry was how the soldiers of the Union army would react.

Between rows of tents, on parade fields, and in the glow of campfires, Union soldiers gathered to discuss the proclamation. They knew that if they refused to fight, then the Confederacy

Horace Greeley

Union soldiers were divided over the effectiveness of the Emancipation Proclamation. Many soldiers resented fighting to abolish slavery, while others saw the proclamation as an inspiration to win the war.

would triumph and the war would end. Their opinions, like those of citizens throughout the country, were passionately divided. One soldier expressed his dismay about the proclamation in a letter to his family, "I am as much in favor for the Union as any one but I am not in favor of shedding my blood for the sake of slaves." An officer complained that the document "has done more harm than good."

Though the proclamation disappointed some Union soldiers, it inspired others. One soldier wrote, "Thank the Lord for this! I hope that this will open a way whereby the Lord can lay his blessing on our arms and give us victory!" Officer Regis de Trebriand stated, "It was no longer a question of the Union *as it was* . . . it was the Union *as it should be.* The war was ennobled; the object [reason for fighting] was higher."

As the year 1862 ended, the world wondered if Lincoln would really make the proclamation law. On New Year's Day 1863, the president kept the promise he had made in September. Surrounded by newspaper reporters, dignitaries, and important officials, Lincoln took a pen from his desk and signed the proclamation. He knew that many Union soldiers did not approve, but he felt confident that the army would not fall apart. Lincoln also had other aims in writing the proclamation. He hoped to damage the Confederate cause not only in North America, but throughout the world.

President Lincoln signed the Emancipation Proclamation on January 1, 1863.

News of the proclamation made a tremendous impact in Europe. At the beginning of the Civil War, many leaders in Europe supported the American South. They believed that the South was defending its right to be independent from the Union. England and France waited for the chance to intervene in the war and force a peaceful resolution between the Confederacy and the United States. But after the Emancipation Proclamation, it appeared that the South was defending slavery. European public support for the proclamation was enormous. In a letter from England, a group of workers wrote that they "joyfully honor" President Lincoln "for your belief in the words of your great founders." France and England refused to give the Confederacy money or weapons. They did not want to support a government that fought to keep people enslaved. The leaders of the Confederacy were disappointed. They had hoped that England or France would help the South's bid for independence. Now that hope was gone.

In this cartoon from a London newspaper, the South is depicted as a man (left) who defies the emancipation being delivered to the slaves by the Union (depicted by an eagle).

Despite Europe's decision to avoid the conflict, the Civil War still raged in the summer of 1864. It had been eighteen months since Lincoln signed the proclamation. The Union and Confederate armies stood opposite each other in southern Virginia, each side exhausted after several bloody battles. Washington, D.C., became so crowded with wounded Union soldiers that doctors were forced to use churches as hospitals. Even the Rotunda in the Capitol building became a temporary shelter. People in the North were tired of the war, and Lincoln was in despair. Many people advised Lincoln to give up the Emancipation Proclamation, hoping that the Southern states would then make peace and return to the Union.

The war took a disastrous toll on armies from both the North and the South.

Lincoln replied, "Should I do so, I should deserve to be damned through time and eternity." Lincoln's response demonstrated how the war had affected him. When he became president in 1861, he was prepared to preserve slavery in order to save the Union. After three years of war, however, Lincoln believed that slavery must be destroyed for the war to end, and for the Union to be saved.

By February 1865, the Confederacy neared collapse. Union armies marched deep into the South, capturing cities and liberating slaves. The border states accepted that slavery was doomed. In Washington, D.C., Lincoln worked with Congress to abolish slavery throughout the United States. In February, Congress passed the Thirteenth Amendment to the Constitution, which made slavery illegal.

Columbia, South Carolina (left), and Atlanta, Georgia (right), were among the cities left in ruins as the Union armies defeated the South.

In celebration, a cheerful crowd of people gathered on the White House lawn and called for President Lincoln to give a speech. Lincoln addressed them from a window. He felt jubilant about the amendment. "It winds the whole thing up," he said. "I congratulate myself, the country, and the whole world upon this great moral victory." Lincoln was even more thrilled when news arrived that on April 9, 1865, General Robert E. Lee and the Confederate army had surrendered to General Ulysses S. Grant, commander of the Union forces, at Appomattox Court House, Virginia. The Civil War was over.

On December 18, 1865, the Thirteenth Amendment formally became part of the U.S. Constitution. Sadly, Lincoln never saw this

The Civil War officially ended when General Robert E. Lee (right) surrendered the Confederate troops to Union General Ulysses S. Grant (left) at Appomattox Court House, Virginia.

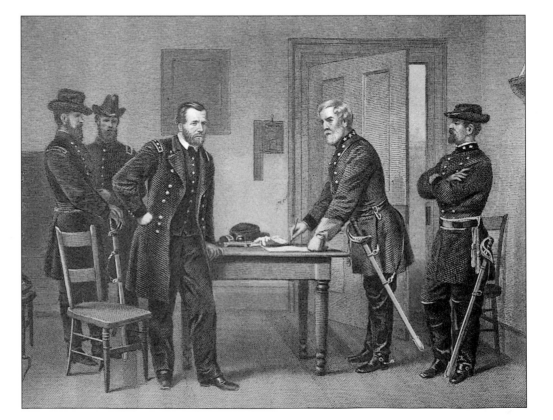

triumph. He had been assassinated on April 15, 1865, eight months before the amendment became law.

President Abraham Lincoln wrote the Emancipation Proclamation because he wanted to end the Civil War. He knew that the document would give the Union army black soldiers, deprive the South of slave workers, and gain the support of European countries. But Lincoln's document did more than just preserve the United States as a union, it saved the United States as a free society. Lincoln believed that a society that allowed slavery was not truly free at all. The Emancipation Proclamation changed the Civil War from a war about unity to a war about democracy. With the South's defeat in 1865, the United States became more free and more equal for all of its people.

President Lincoln was shot while attending a theater performance on April 14, 1865. He died early the next day, surrounded by his wife, his doctors, his cabinet members, and his close friends.

At the time the proclamation was issued, Lincoln told Congress, "In giving freedom to the slave, we assure freedom for the free." No longer would the United States be a society of contradiction. No longer would a country that claimed freedom for all of its citizens keep men, women, and children in chains.

Abraham Lincoln understood the significance of the Emancipation Proclamation. While signing it on January 1, 1863, Lincoln confidently stated, "If I go down in history, it will be for this act."

Lincoln is indeed remembered as the man who

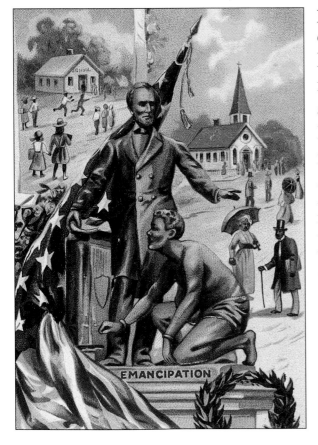

In this idealized version of Emancipation, Lincoln frees the slaves. But many slaves freed themselves by escaping either to join the Union army or rebuild their lives in Northern cities.

EMANCIPATION

presided over one of the worst conflicts in United States history, but his presidency is memorable for other accomplishments as well. The Homestead Act, which granted free family farms to settlers, and the Land Grant Act, which provided for the sale of public land for agricultural education, were both approved in 1862. The Land Grant Act eventually led to the establishment of state universities. Lincoln also signed the Railroad Act in 1862, which provided for the building of the United States's first transcontinental railroad.

Abraham Lincoln is today recognized as one of the greatest leaders in the history of the United States.

Abraham Lincoln is considered to be one of the most beloved presidents ever to hold this country's highest office. He continues to be admired for the same qualities that were praised by writers for the *Washington Chronicle* while the Civil War still raged: ". . . great calmness of temper, great firmness of purpose, supreme moral principle, and intense patriotism."

GLOSSARY

William Seward was a member of Lincoln's cabinet.

cabinet – group of advisors for the head of a government

Capitol – building where the United States Congress meets

Congress – the part of the United States government that is responsible for making laws; made up of the Senate and the House of Representatives

dignitary – person who holds an important or honored position

emancipate – to free a person or group from slavery or control

ennoble – to make something more important by focusing on its ideals or morals

garrison – a military post; a central location where many soldiers are located

immoral – unfair; without a sense of what is right and what is wrong

jubilant – very happy and full of joy

liberate – to set someone free

proclamation – document or declaration

recruit – person who has recently joined the military

regiment – military unit

Rotunda – the large central area under the dome of the Capitol building

wary – uncertain or cautious

regiment

TIMELINE

1787 U.S. Constitution adopted

Northern factories employ immigrants, Southern plantations use slaves **1800**

Abolitionists begin to oppose slavery **1830**

1860

1861

February: Confederate States of America forms

April: Civil War begins

November: Abraham Lincoln elected President

December: South Carolina secedes from Union

May: Union attempt to end war fails

July: Lincoln reads proclamation to cabinet

September: Union army drives Confederates out of Maryland Lincoln reads proclamation to public

1862

1863 *January:* Lincoln signs proclamation into law

1865 *April:* Civil War ends, Lincoln assassinated
December: Thirteenth Amendment passed

INDEX (*Boldface page numbers indicate illustrations.*)

ABOUT THE AUTHOR

Brendan January was born and raised in Pleasantville, New York. He attended Haverford College in Pennsylvania, where he earned his B.A. in History and English. An Abraham Lincoln enthusiast, he has written three books for the Cornerstones of Freedom series, *The Emancipation Proclamation, Fort Sumter,* and *The Lincoln-Douglas Debates.* Mr. January divides his time between New York City and Danbury, Connecticut.